About the Author

Abigail Rundblom is a writer, artist, and molecular biologist originally from Illinois. She has a bachelor's in animal science and a master's in agricultural education and leadership studies from the University of Illinois at Urbana-Champaign. She began a Ph.D. program in pathobiology but decided to pursue writing as it was her first passion. Abigail currently resides in the Fargo-Moorhead region of North Dakota and Minnesota. *Midnight Afternoons* is her first publication.

Midnight Afternoons

Abigail Rundblom

Midnight Afternoons

Vanguard Press

VANGUARD PAPERBACK

© Copyright 2024
Abigail Rundblom

The right of Abigail Rundblom to be identified as author of this work has been asserted by her in accordance with the Copyright, Designs and Patents Act 1988.

All Rights Reserved

No reproduction, copy, or transmission of this publication may be made without written permission.
No paragraph of this publication may be reproduced, copied or transmitted save with the written permission of the publisher, or in accordance with the provisions of the Copyright Act 1956 (as amended).

Any person who commits any unauthorised act in relation to this publication may be liable to criminal prosecution and civil claims for damages.

A CIP catalogue record for this title is available from the British Library.

ISBN 978-1-83794-299-2

This is a work of fiction. Names, characters, businesses, places, events, and incidents are either the products of the author's imagination or used in a fictitious manner. Any resemblance to actual persons, living or dead, or actual events is purely coincidental.

Vanguard Press is an imprint of
Pegasus Elliot Mackenzie Publishers Ltd.
www.pegasuspublishers.com

First Published in 2024

Vanguard Press
Sheraton House Castle Park
Cambridge England

Printed & Bound in Great Britain

Dedication

For Ash, Bri, David, Dr. Fergie, and Holly who supported and loved me through some of my darkest days.

A.M.

I hate to think you didn't love me.
The thought is unbearable.
I saw the pain in your eyes
every morning we met.
A boy who lost his father, his way.
His love for life
buried somewhere deep,
unable to unearth.
I hate to think you didn't love me.
I'm certain you had to.
Or how could you?
Your touch was rough,
yet young, naïve,
despite the years
the universe put between us.
I hate to think you didn't love me.
But I saw it in your eyes.
Along with the pain,
confliction, confusion.
Holding me,
am I a daughter, a lover,
a friend?
I hate to think you didn't love me.
I'm happy to know you still do.

X

Did you mean to do it?
Surely not.

How could anyone?
Be so cold, calculated.
The love drug,
once on my tongue,
I couldn't rid myself of the taste.
You caressed my body,
my soul that evening.
Holding my waist
between two clammy palms.
You had a grip.
So tight.
So gentle.
Tracing the hallucinated checkerboard on my exposed
skin.
A sigh.
Kissed every inch of my body
until the water draped over us.
I washed your hair,
breathed you in,
for our last moment of peace.

A Carving I

March is for healing.
The wounds you left were jagged, rigid,
senselessly bloody.
Carved with a serrated knife
I could tell you used before.
Dull and unclean,
you tore into me.
"Are you falling for me?"
"No?"
Dig deeper,
until we scrape bone,
slicing every nerve on the way.
"Do you want me now?"
"Yes?"
I have you.
Now twist.
Carelessly,
violently,
pull.
One swift motion,
leaving nothing to slow the bleeding.

April

I don't think you could tell me why, even if you tried.
You care? How?
You want me? Why?
You don't try.
You never will.
Nothing but a laugh.
A plaything.
I don't think you could tell me why, even if you tried.

July

It always ended as quickly as it started.
A moth to a flame.
A child running back to his mother.
Scared, lonely, afraid.

"Do you know how much I care about you?"

"No?"

You cling to my leg,
gripping tightly.

Only a short time
until you're lost again.

Firestorm

A hit never felt like a kiss,
but betrayal often did.

Choking, sweating, gasping for air.

No.

These worldly pains never felt like a kiss,
but betrayal often did.

Lunera I

Interesting
how you
managed
to get
away with it.
A short phone call
was enough
to absolve your sins.
I was fifteen when Lunera
materialized,
fifteen when it began.
You'll never understand,
believe
the pain you caused.
But maybe,
there is some hope.
When you look
at the moon,
you're reminded
of me.

Prairie Meadows

I wore flannel to be like you,
but I never wanted you inside of me.
Funny how we held hands
in a park I didn't recognize.
What was familiar to you was foreign to me.
What was familiar to me was foreign to you.

I wore flannel to be like you,
but I never wanted you inside of me.
Funny how we kissed
in a bar far from home.
Unrecognizable to both.
I wore flannel to be like you,
but I never wanted you inside of me.

We finally paused.
A break in the madness.

Too little,
too late.
You were inside of me.

Carle

I couldn't let you die like that.
Alone.
In a cage,
speaking to your father.
I cannot,
will not
remember how you looked that evening.
Naked.
Reaching toward the sky,
toward anything tangible.

Your father.
Your mother.
Death.
Anything.
I couldn't,
I refused
to let you die like that.

Cool Center

Too raw.
Too emotional.
Undercooked,
visceral.
Bloody,
tender,
blue.

Love was too much for you,
too strong of a word.
I can't,
I won't,
I refuse to
believe you didn't love me too.

Summer of Five

The 1970s floral print monster
calmly watched
in the corner of his dark room.
The room with cheap cotton curtains now always
associated with discomfort.
It was always hot in the summers. Peeling clothes off the
body. Panting with thirst.
Sprinklers to stay wet.
Summer was the season.
Poking at the past with a jagged stick, rummaging.
Until remembering something inescapable.
The monster always comes back. It never left.
Always lingering.
A touch, word, season, number.

Summer

Five.
Bury it. Drown it.
But there was light in healing, and she would find it.

Enough

We were at war.
You had your witnesses; I had mine.
A testament to your character?
The manipulation,
abuse.
A testament to my character?
"They don't give a shit who you are."
We were at war. Was this new?
We've been at war since the first A.M.
Dark,
damp.
You pushed me against the wall,
kissed me hungrily.

Only then,
I was not yet able to say,
enough.

XII

I woke up thinking of you.
I thought you were with me.
I couldn't explain it.
You were my body;
I was yours.
You meant everything to me.
I meant nothing to you.

Forever connected,
destined to fall apart.

Ankh

Holding me
on the couch
in front of George.
He was concerned.
You weren't.
I was.

I'm sure we smelled off to him.
He growled.
You gripped me harder.
In your arms, I thought you a savior.
You proved to be nothing more than another demon.

A Carving II

August is for healing.
The wounds I allowed you to leave were jagged,
rigid,
senselessly bloody.
Carved with a serrated knife
I could tell you used before.
Dull and unclean,
you tore into me.
"Will you stay for me?"

"No?"

Again, digging deeper,
scraping bone,
slicing every nerve on the way.

"You'll stay now."

"Yes."
Twist.
Carelessly,
violently,
pull.
One swift motion.

Only now,
I stop the bleeding.

October

Strolling the florescent halls,
I often thought of you.
Thinking it would be something.
Joyful
with new beginnings.
Virgin,
green.

But this is fall,
novel beginnings tossed aside.

Leaves gathering,
decaying.
Relieved
when they burned.

December

Last time in the desert,
a destitute conversation.
Again,
wanting me briefly.
I *always* come back.
The cacti were far less prickly
than your general disposition.
I always *came* back.
The darkness fell,
bats flew,
and I thought I left you there.

Maine

xx
Here I am,
across the fucking country, thinking about you.
God, I have it bad.
xx

Lunera II

As the
inappropriate
messages
you frequently sent
are over
ten years old,
there is no legal action
I can or will take.
I sincerely hope the
wildly inappropriate
relationships
you had
with your high school
students started and ended
with me.
Though I
will never
understand why,
I forgive
you.

Dust

I believed it to be
the beginning of a new chapter.
Lush and green.
Budding in spring with fresh growth.
Moonflowers?
Garden in the alley?

Now, nothing but broken glass,
disillusioned allure.

The promise of new beginnings,
dashed,
shredded into the
normal bullshit.

Not knowing or understanding,
how to be loved.

Null

I apologize for Friday.
I can assure you,
it will not happen again.
Should have been avoided.

Though I still believe meeting to be beneficial, bottom
line is,
I need this to be completely, permanently,
done.
Please.

No more texting when you're high and sentimental.
No more waiting to find what you want.
Just over.
I'm begging you to let me go.

Coming from previous abusive relationships, your
behavior
is triggering.
Why do you keep doing this?

We're not bad people; this is a fucked situation that keeps
getting worse.
You're fucking horrible.

I would like to remain cordial and friendly,
as I'm sure we'll see each other out.
Let me know when you read this.
You won't.

I hope you find happiness.
I know I will without you.

Hedge Ball Hunting

I recall the creek most vividly.
Flooding in the spring, often taking days to recede.
I realized much later,
I would express my emotions in a similar fashion.
Spilling,
overflowing,
until the ground soaked up my anger,
confusion,
blame.
I threw hedge balls into this creek.
Adding people to my story.
Though they'd float,
it was still raging waters
no one could navigate better than you.

Campfire

Is there anything more satisfying than starting a fire?
In love,
friendship,
lust.
Trouble is
burning too quickly.
So, tend to your fires,
as though they're delicate seedlings.
Fragile,
requiring constant care.
With proper
time,
adequate kindling,
they may grow and burn eternally.

Dragonflies

"Oh, hi guys."
What?
"Two dragonflies, together, landed on me."
"Ope. Now they're drinking water off me."
How easily you changed your mind,
your personality.
"Now he's washing his face."
I only wish you would have shared such tenderness with
me.
"Go away, you two."
Back to familiarity.

2022

Ah,
the soothing sounds of logging.
Swimming in crystal clear water.
Dreaming of a simple country life.
Buzzing,
whirring,
beeping.

With an enormous thud,
one tree hitting the ground,
Reality.

Morchella

Of course,
time is not linear.
Have you not seen your birth,
your death?
Don't worry.
We exist indefinitely.

Too Much

I was bobbing
up and down
with a broken record player in the ocean.
You sat on the porch with me.
Oddly enough,
your hand on my waist.
I had just died.
Old faithful was the savior.
You were
more concerned you'd lose the sex
than me.
Then you wondered why I left.

Floating

She told me it was an imagined future:
"The future you want with him doesn't exist.
It never will."
She was right.
I loved her more, far more
than I could
ever love him.
She was right, and I left.

Dakotas

I tried to shake you,
but you were stuck on me.

Like the mud and shit
of the horses behind your office.

I take a deep breath,
and you're there
behind me,
savagely grabbing my waist
as the water sloshes into
the bath.

Hung like a field mouse
in a South Dakota blizzard,
you'd joke.

Well, I'm in North Dakota now,
and I hoped to God
you wouldn't find me here.
But you did.
I feel you everywhere.
Even now,
I cannot shake you.

P.M.

By early afternoon,
you had gone.

I only served you
in the early morning hours.

When it was dark,
and we were both vulnerable.

I don't think you could face me
in the daylight.

You knew the pain you were
causing and had caused
many times before
with many different women.

But I was different,
and you were afraid.

As it turns out,
you had every right to be.

I was different,
and I stopped you in your tracks.

Printed in the USA
CPSIA information can be obtained
at www.ICGtesting.com
LVHW041304051124
795735LV00004BA/562